THE ULTIMATE GUIDE TO FUSION 360: 2024 EDITION

CHAPTER 1: DIVE INTO FUSION 360 – THE BEGINNER'S MANUAL

1.1 Getting Started with Fusion 360

Before we make the digital canvas our playground, let's get acquainted with the basics.

Installation and Setup:
Head over to the Autodesk website and sign up for an account.
Download Fusion 360 based on your operating system (Windows/Mac).
Run the installer and follow on-screen instructions.

1.2 Exploring the User Interface

Fusion 360's user interface might look intimidating at first, but don't sweat it! Let's break it down.

Navigating the Workspace:
Top Toolbar: Contains tools organized by functionality – sketch, create, modify, etc.
Left Panel: Your browser – lists all components, bodies, and sketches.
ViewCube: Located on the top-right – click and drag to rotate your model.

1.3 Starting Your First Sketch

You can't build without a blueprint, and in Fusion 360, that's your sketch.

Choosing a Plane:

Click on 'Create Sketch' in the top toolbar.
Select a plane (front, top, or right).
Using Basic Sketch Tools:

Line Tool: Click to start, click to end. Easy!
Rectangle Tool: Click once for the first corner, drag, then click for the opposite corner.
Circle Tool: Click for the center, drag for the radius, then release.
1.4 Turning Sketches into 3D Models

This is where the magic happens!

Extruding:

Click on your sketch to select it.
Choose 'Extrude' from the top toolbar.
Drag the arrow or type in a distance. Boom, 3D!
Revolving:

Ideal for cylindrical objects.
Select your sketch, then choose 'Revolve'.
Pick an axis (like a line in your sketch) to revolve around.
1.5 Modifying Your Model

Made a mistake or want to jazz things up? No worries!

Chamfers and Fillets:

Choose the 'Chamfer' or 'Fillet' tool.
Click on an edge of your model.
Drag or type in a value. Look at those smooth edges!
Holes and Patterns:

Use the 'Hole' tool for... well, making holes!
'Pattern' lets you repeat features like holes or extrusions. Super handy!
1.6 Saving and Organizing Your Work

No one likes lost work, so let's keep things tidy!

Saving Your File:

Click on the floppy disk icon (or File > Save).
Give your masterpiece a name.
Organizing Projects:

On the left, you'll see a 'Data Panel'. Click it.
Create folders to group related projects. Like "Rocket Designs" or "Cool Stuff I Made".

CHAPTER 2: ADVANCED SKETCHING AND CONSTRAINTS - UNLOCKING THE TRUE POTENTIAL

2.1 Diving Deeper into Sketching Tools

Now that you're no longer a rookie, let's up our game!

Polygons and Splines:
Polygons: Found under the 'Sketch' dropdown. You can create hexagons, pentagons, or any "-gons" you like!
Splines: Curvy lines that flow smoothly. Click for each point and watch the magic curve appear.
2.2 Constraints: The Glue of Your Sketch

Constraints ensure your sketch behaves the way you want. Like setting rules for misbehaving crayons.

Coincident:

Makes points sit on top of each other or on a line. It's like telling two points to hold hands!
Tangential:

Makes curves touch straight lines or other curves just right, ensuring they're best friends but not too clingy.
Horizontal/Vertical:

Keeps lines straight up or straight across. No slouching lines here!
2.3 Utilizing Offset and Trim Tools

Your sketch won't always be perfect. But with these tools, perfection is just a few clicks away!

Offset:

Select the 'Offset' tool and then a line or shape.
Drag in or out to create a parallel copy. It's like your sketch's shadow!
Trim:

With the 'Trim' tool, click on any unnecessary or extra lines.
Watch the excess just melt away. Ah, satisfaction!
2.4 Advanced Revolving and Lofting

Let's move into 3D with style!

Lofting Between Sketches:
Create two or more sketches on different planes.
With 'Loft', select these sketches, and Fusion will create a smooth transition between them. It's like connecting the dots, but in 3D!
2.5 Mirroring and Patterning in Sketch

Double the fun without the effort!

Mirroring:

Draw half of your design.
Using the 'Mirror' tool, select your lines and choose a mirror line.
Voila, the other half magically appears!
Patterning:

Choose 'Rectangular' or 'Circular' pattern in the sketch menu.
Select the sketch elements you want to pattern and set the

direction or axis. Watch your design multiply!

2.6 Parametric Design: Using Parameters

Let's introduce math to design, making changes a breeze!

Setting Parameters:
Under 'Modify', choose 'Change Parameters'.
Create named values (like "Width" or "Height") and use them in your sketches.
Adjust the values, and your design updates automatically. It's like magic, but it's math!

CHAPTER 3: ASSEMBLIES AND COMPONENTS - MAKING PARTS PLAY NICE

3.1 Understanding the Basics of Assemblies

Assemblies are when multiple bodies come together for a party in your project.

Why Assemblies?:
This allows multiple components to interact in one space. Think of it as having a bunch of toy cars and seeing how they all fit inside a toy garage.
3.2 Creating and Managing Components

Components are individual parts. Like a bolt, a wheel, or even a fancy gear.

Creating a New Component:

In the Browser, right-click on the top-level file name.
Select "New Component". Name it something snazzy.
Activate the component by clicking on the little circle next to its name. This tells Fusion 360, "Hey, I'm working on THIS now!"
Why Components?:

It's all about organization. Each component can have its own sketches, bodies, and even other components.

3.3 Joint and Motion Studies

Let's get things moving!

Using Joints:

Click the 'Joint' button under 'Assemble'.
Pick the two parts you want to join.
Choose from various types like "revolute" or "slider". It's like deciding how two parts should dance together!
Motion Studies:

After setting your joints, click 'Animate Joints' to see how they move. Watch them break it down on the digital dance floor!

3.4 Inserting Components and External Files

Don't reinvent the wheel. Or the bolt. Or that super complex gear you made last week.

Inserting a Component:
Under 'Insert', select 'Insert into Current Design'.
Choose the component or file.
Click OK, and bam! Your component is now part of the party.

3.5 Component Color Cycling

Lost in a sea of components? Let's add some color!

Using Color Cycling:
Right-click in the canvas.
Choose 'Component Color Cycling Toggle'.
Now, each component has its own color. It's like assigning everyone at the party a flashy, unique hat!

CHAPTER 4: MATERIALS, APPEARANCES, AND PHYSICS - ADDING SOME PIZZAZZ

4.1 Spicing Up Your Designs with Materials

Because who doesn't want their designs to look snazzy?

Assigning Materials:
Click on the 'Physical Material' from the 'Modify' dropdown.
Drag and drop your desired material onto the component. Steel, gold, wood – you name it!
4.2 Customizing Appearances

Beyond just materials, appearances add texture, reflections, and transparency.

Using Appearances:
Right-click on your component.
Select 'Appearance'. A beautiful palette appears!
Choose an effect or texture, like brushed metal or frosted glass. You're an artist, after all!
4.3 Real-world Physics with Simulation Studies

Let's put your designs to the test!

Setting up a Study:

Under the 'Simulation' workspace, select 'Study'.
Choose a type: static stress, thermal effects, etc.
Assign constraints and loads. Tell Fusion where it's fixed, where it's pushed, or if it's feeling the heat!
Analyzing Results:

After running the study, Fusion provides a visual representation of stresses, displacements, and more. Colorful, and oh-so-enlightening!
4.4 Tinkering with Tolerances

Because in design, even 0.1mm can make a world of difference!

Setting Tolerances:
Under 'Inspect', click 'Tolerance Analysis'.
Define your maximum and minimum values. This tells Fusion, "Hey, keep it between these lines!"
Review how these tolerances affect assembly fits and function.
4.5 Making it Shine with Rendering

All that hard work deserves to be showcased in the best light!

Starting a Render:
Switch to the 'Render' workspace.
Adjust the scene settings: lighting, background, camera angle.
Click 'Render'. Fusion works its magic, and voilà, a masterpiece!

CHAPTER 5: MANUFACTURING AND COLLABORATION - MAKING IDEAS TANGIBLE

5.1 Dive into CAM (Computer-Aided Manufacturing)

Turn those designs into real, tangible items!

CAM Workspace Basics:
Toggle to the 'CAM' workspace.
Here, you can define operations like milling, turning, and cutting.
Set up your machine, tool, and material. Fusion's like, "Okay, boss, let's carve this masterpiece!"
5.2 Toolpaths – The Roadmap of Your Machine

Guide your machines with grace and precision!

Defining a Toolpath:
Choose an operation like '2D Pocket' or '3D Adaptive Clearing'.
Select your tool, speeds, and feeds.
Preview the path. See that tool dance across your design!
5.3 Post Processing – Chatting with Machines

Because machines need their specific lingo!

How to Post Process:
Once your toolpaths are set, hit the 'Post Process' button.
Select your machine's language (G-code format).
Save and transfer to your CNC machine. It's chit-chat time!
5.4 Team Collaboration – Because Two Heads are Better!

Share, discuss, and make design dreams come true together!

Using Fusion Team:
Click on the 'Team' button.
Invite members by their email. Welcome to the party, pals!
Comment, markup, and review designs in real-time. Virtual brainstorming FTW!
5.5 Version Control – Time Travel in Fusion

Mistakes happen, but fear not, Fusion's got a time machine!

Accessing Version History:
In the Data Panel, right-click on your design.
Select 'Version History'.
View, restore, or compare versions. Blast from the past!

CHAPTER 6: ADVANCED DESIGN TECHNIQUES & OPTIMIZATION - UNLEASHING YOUR FUSION SUPERPOWERS

6.1 Parametric Modeling – Make Changes on the Fly

Flexibility is the name of the game!

Setting Up Parameters:
Go to the 'Modify' dropdown and select 'Change Parameters'.
Add user parameters like length, width, and height.
Attach these parameters to your design elements. Now, update in one place, see changes everywhere!
6.2 Sculpting – Get Artistic with T-Splines

Embrace your inner sculptor!

Diving into Sculpt Workspace:
Switch to the 'Sculpt' workspace.
Start with primitives like spheres or boxes.

Push, pull, and twist those T-spline faces. Create organic, flowing designs effortlessly!

6.3 Sheet Metal – Bending it Right

For when you need to get a bit more...metallic.

Beginning with Sheet Metal:
Jump into the 'Sheet Metal' workspace.
Create flanges, bends, and folds.
Use the 'Flat Pattern' feature to see how your design will look unfolded. Perfect for laser cutting!

6.4 Topological Optimization – When Less is More

Make your designs strong but lightweight!

Starting Optimization:
Head to 'Simulation' workspace and choose 'Shape Optimization'.
Define loads, constraints, and objectives.
Let Fusion analyze and recommend material reductions. Efficiency at its best!

6.5 Animation – Bring Your Design to Life

Because moving things are just cooler!

Animating Your Assemblies:
In the 'Animation' workspace, drag the timeline slider.
Set up actions like move, rotate, or fade.
Play it back. Voilà, your design is alive and kicking!

CHAPTER 7: FUSION 360 IN THE REAL WORLD - INDUSTRIES, APPLICATIONS, AND INSPIRATION

7.1 Automotive Design – The Future on Wheels

Crafting sleek, aerodynamic beasts for the roads!

Sketching a Car Chassis:
Use the 'Sketch' mode and lay out the car's side profile.
Extrude and loft surfaces for the body.
Add intricate details like grilles, headlights, and tires. Your vehicle's ready to vroom!
7.2 Architecture & Infrastructure – Constructing Tomorrow

Building the metropolises of the future!

Designing a Skyscraper:
Start with the floor plan in 'Sketch'.
Extrude each level, ensuring structural consistency.
Incorporate windows, terraces, and facades. You've just designed the next iconic landmark!
7.3 Product Design – Innovations for Everyday

Creating objects that change lives daily!

Sketching a Smartwatch:
Kick off with the watch's face and straps.
Use 'Sculpt' for a sleek, ergonomic finish.
Add functional elements: buttons, screen, sensors. It's tech, fashion, and innovation, all in one!
7.4 Aerospace – To Infinity and Beyond!

Designing crafts that reach for the stars!

Modeling a Drone:
Begin with the central body, considering aerodynamics.
Add propellers, ensuring balance and symmetry.
Incorporate camera mounts and sensors. Ready for takeoff!
7.5 Wearable Tech – Fusion Fashion Forward

Tech that you wear, making everyday chic and smart!

Creating Smart Glasses:
Design a stylish frame using 'Sketch' and 'Sculpt'.
Embed tech elements: mini screens, cameras, and sensors.
Ensure ergonomic fit. Function meets fashion in a seamless blend!

CHAPTER 8: SIMULATING AND TESTING - ENSURING PERFECTION IN EVERY PIXEL

8.1 Structural Analysis - Standing Strong

Let's ensure your designs can bear the weight of expectations!

Setting Up a Structural Test:
Enter the 'Simulation' workspace.
Select the fixed and load-bearing points of your design.
Apply pressures and forces, then run the simulation. Interpret the color-coded results to understand stress points and optimize accordingly.
8.2 Thermal Analysis - Hot or Not?

For those designs that might break a sweat.

Conducting a Thermal Test:
Still in 'Simulation', opt for 'Thermal Stress'.
Input heat sources and define cooling conditions.
Simulate to see how your design reacts to temperature changes.
Adjust materials or design features based on outcomes.
8.3 Fluid Dynamics - Go with the Flow

For all things liquid and gaseous.

Simulating Fluid Flow:
Choose 'Fluid Dynamics' in the simulation suite.
Define the fluid's properties and the paths it'll take.
Run the simulation. Observe flow rates and turbulence, and refine the design for smoother flow.
8.4 Motion Studies - Move It, Move It!

Let's ensure those moving parts groove in harmony.

Setting Up a Motion Study:
Head to 'Motion Study' in 'Simulation'.
Define joints, constraints, and movements.
Watch your design parts move in sync. Adjust for any clashing or misalignments.
8.5 CAM & Manufacturing - Making it Real

Time to get it out of the screen and into the world.

Setting Up for Manufacturing:
Switch to the 'CAM' workspace.
Choose the right tool paths for cutting, drilling, or milling.
Simulate the manufacturing process, refining tool paths for efficiency and accuracy.

CHAPTER 9: INTEGRATION AND COLLABORATION - FUSION 360 IN THE ECOSYSTEM

9.1 CAD Software Integration - Smooth Transitions

No more compatibility headaches. Fusion 360 to the rescue!

Importing from Other CAD Platforms:
In the 'File' menu, select 'Import'.
Choose your file format, be it .DWG, .DXF, or any other.
Check for any inconsistencies post-import and use 'Tweak' to fix.
And voilà! Perfectly ported design.
9.2 Cloud Collaboration - Teamwork in the Sky

Harness the cloud. Bring your dream team on board.

Setting Up Cloud Collaboration:
Click on the 'Share' icon in the top right.
Invite team members via their emails.
Set permissions and watch as changes synchronize in real-time.
Fusion 360's cloud: where design dreams and team streams converge.
9.3 Plugin Play - Boosting Fusion's Power

There's a plugin for everything. Seriously.

Installing a New Plugin:
Head to the 'Add-ins' tab.
Click on 'Scripts and Add-ins'.
Browse the library or upload a custom plugin. Activate, and let the magic unfold.
9.4 Real-Time Rendering - See It to Believe It

Because waiting is so last century.

Initiating a Render:
Transition to the 'Render' workspace.
Pick materials, lighting, and backgrounds.
Hit 'In-Canvas Render'. In moments, watch your design come alive in photorealistic glory.
9.5 Feedback and Annotation - Constructive Conversations

Get feedback. Iterate. Perfect.

Adding Comments:
Select the 'Comment' tab on the right.
Click a point on your design.
Type your feedback. Collaborators can view and respond. Design democracy at its finest!

CHAPTER 10: THE FUTURE OF FUSION 360 - EMBRACING TOMORROW'S INNOVATIONS

10.1 AI in Fusion - Smarter Designing

Fusion 360's flirting with AI, and it's a match made in tech heaven!

Leveraging Design AI:
Access the 'AI Tools' pane.
Engage 'Design Suggestions'. Feed it parameters, and let AI brainstorm with you.
Review AI-generated designs. Iterate, refine, and decide.
10.2 Augmented Reality (AR) - Virtual Becomes Reality

Fuse the real world with your designs.

Setting Up an AR View:
Navigate to the 'Render' workspace.
Click 'AR Mode'.
Scan your environment with an AR-compatible device. Place your design, scale, and explore in augmented glory.
10.3 Advanced Materials - Beyond the Basics

Research, model, and apply cutting-edge materials.

Accessing Advanced Materials:
Under 'Materials Library', click 'Advanced'.
Browse material properties and applications.
Assign to your design, harnessing the power of next-gen materials.

10.4 Quantum Computing Integration - Processing at Lightspeed

Jumping into the quantum realm for unparalleled computation.

Engaging Quantum Tools:
In the 'Tools' menu, select 'Quantum Simulation'.
Input parameters and execute simulations leveraging quantum mechanics.
Analyze results for ultra-accurate, ultra-fast insights.

10.5 Eco-Design and Sustainability - Designing for Earth

Being a superhero for our planet? Yes, please!

Eco-friendly Designing:
Open 'Eco-Design Toolkit'.
Evaluate your design's environmental footprint.
Implement eco-friendly suggestions, decreasing waste and optimizing resource use.

CHAPTER 11: MASTERING COLLABORATION IN FUSION 360

11.1 The Fusion Team - Together Everyone Achieves More

No one's an island; Fusion 360 gets that!

Setting Up Your Team:
Access 'File' and select 'New Team'.
Assign members by adding their email addresses.
Assign roles: Viewer, Editor, or Admin.
11.2 Real-time Collaboration - Because Waiting is So Last Decade

Create with your squad, wherever they're located.

Initiating a Collaborative Session:
Open the design you want to co-edit.
Click on the 'Collaborate' icon.
Invite members using their Fusion 360 IDs.
11.3 Version Control - A Designer's Time Machine

Ever wish you had a time machine? Fusion's got your back!

Accessing Previous Versions:
In the 'Data Panel', right-click on your project.
Select 'Version History'.
Browse through the timeline, view changes, and revert if

necessary.

11.4 Commenting and Annotation - Because Communication is Key

Speak your design mind!

Leaving Feedback:
In the design space, click on the area you want to comment on.
Select 'Add Comment'.
Type your thoughts, and mention team members using '@'.

11.5 Shared Link Views - Showcase Without Sharing Everything

Protect your intellectual property while flexing your genius.

Setting Up a Shared View:
Click on 'Share' in the top-right corner.
Select 'Create Link'.
Adjust view permissions and send the link to partners, clients, or your mom (she'll be proud).

CHAPTER 12: SIMULATION & VALIDATION - MAKING SURE YOUR DESIGNS DON'T JUST LOOK COOL

12.1 Introduction to Simulation in Fusion 360

Because guessing is so medieval!

Accessing Simulation Workbench:
Navigate to the workspaces dropdown.
Select 'Simulation'.
Familiarize yourself with the environment; it's your sandbox!

12.2 Structural Analysis - Holding It Together

Is your design strong enough? Let's find out!

Initiating a Structural Analysis:
In the 'Simulation' workspace, click 'Structural Analysis'.
Define fixed points, loads, and materials.
Run the analysis and examine the stress points.

12.3 Thermal Analysis - Feeling the Heat?

For when you need to know if your design can take the heat... or cold!

Setting Up a Thermal Analysis:
Click 'Thermal Analysis' in the 'Simulation' workspace.
Assign heat sources and sinks.
Analyze how your design handles temperature changes.
12.4 Modal Frequencies - Shake, Rattle, and Roll

Ensure your design won't shake itself apart.

Performing Modal Analysis:
Select 'Modal Frequencies' in the 'Simulation' workspace.
Assign constraints and loads.
Identify natural frequencies and potential vibration issues.
12.5 Fluid Dynamics - Going with the Flow

A design might be solid, but how does it interact with fluids?

Running a Fluid Dynamics Test:
Click 'Fluid Flow' in the 'Simulation' workspace.
Define fluid properties and flow rates.
Examine how fluids navigate around or within your design.

CHAPTER 13: RENDERING & VISUALIZATION - MAKING YOUR DESIGNS SHINE BRIGHT LIKE A DIAMOND

13.1 Diving into the Rendering Workspace

The difference between "meh" and "WOW"!

Accessing Rendering Workspace:
Go to the workspaces dropdown.
Select 'Render'.
Immerse yourself; this is where your design gets its glam!
13.2 Setting Up Scenes - Stage Your Masterpiece

Everything's about the right ambiance.

Arranging a Scene:
In the 'Scene Settings', select a background or environment.
Adjust the ground plane, ensuring your model is correctly positioned.

Adjust the lighting to create desired shadows and highlights.
13.3 Applying Materials - Because Grey is So 50 Movies Ago

Your design deserves more than a bland hue!

Using Fusion's Material Library:
In the 'Render' workspace, click 'Appearance'.
Browse through materials like metals, plastics, or even fabrics.
Drag and drop your chosen material onto parts of your model.
13.4 Setting Up Camera Angles - Vogue! Strike a Pose

Make your design ready for its magazine cover!

Creating Camera Views:
Navigate to 'Named Views' on the right panel.
Adjust the perspective using orbit, pan, and zoom.
Click 'Save Current View' to capture and revisit that angle anytime.
13.5 Running the Final Render - Lights, Camera, RENDER!

The red carpet moment for your design!

Initiating the Rendering Process:
Once satisfied with materials and scene setup, click 'Render'.
Choose between 'In-canvas' (quick previews) or 'Cloud' (detailed renders).
Sip your coffee and watch Fusion 360 work its magic.

CHAPTER 14: DOCUMENTATION - THE BRIDGE BETWEEN IDEAS AND REALITY

14.1 Setting the Scene for Documentation

Blueprints, meet Fusion 360. Fusion 360, meet blueprints.

Navigating to the Design Workspace:
Head to the workspace dropdown.
This time, choose 'Design'.
Voilà! Welcome to where your creation gets its instruction manual.
14.2 Creating Detailed Drawings - The Designer's Canvas

A picture speaks a thousand words; a detailed drawing? Probably a million.

Initiating a New Drawing:
Right-click on your design name in the browser.
Select 'New Drawing'.
Choose a template: go standard or go rogue with a custom one.
14.3 Projecting Views - Every Angle Matters

Let's see that design from the front, side, top, and even the tricky oblique angles!

Drafting Views:

Click 'Projected View' in the toolbar.

Pick a face or plane as your parent view.

Drag to project secondary views. It's like making design clones!

14.4 Dimensioning and Annotation - Talking the Technical Talk

Size matters! And so does making sure everyone knows those sizes.

Adding Dimensions:

Select 'Dimension' in the toolbar.

Click on the lines or points you want to measure.

Adjust the position and input the value. Precision is the game!

Throwing in Annotations:

Choose 'Text' in the toolbar.

Click where you'd like the annotation to appear.

Type in your wise words, and don't forget: emojis are not standard. ��

14.5 Exporting and Sharing - Spreading the Genius

The world deserves to see (and understand) your brilliance!

Saving as a PDF or DWG:

Right-click on the drawing tab at the bottom.

Select 'Save as'.

Choose your format. Go classic with PDF or stay digital with DWG.

CHAPTER 15: COLLABORATION - TEAMWORK MAKES THE DREAM WORK IN FUSION 360

15.1 Setting the Scene for Team-Based Design

Gather 'round, team! It's time to create together.

Switching to the Team Hub:
At the top-right corner, click on your profile.
Select 'Switch Hub'.
Dive into the team hub! Feel the collective design vibes.
15.2 Inviting Collaborators - More Minds, More Magic

Who said three's a crowd? In Fusion 360, it's a party.

Sharing Your Design:
Open the design you want to share.
Click on the 'Share' icon in the top-right corner.
Choose 'Invite People'. Whip out your contacts list and get inviting!
15.3 Version Control - Avoiding the "Which One's the Final FINAL?" Conundrum

Save yourself from design chaos. Embrace versions.

Creating Versions:

Head over to the 'Data Panel'.

Right-click your design and select 'Create Version'.

Add a detailed description. Trust me; "fixed the thing" won't help in two weeks.

15.4 Leaving Comments - Constructive Feedback FTW

Did you spot something cool? Or quirky? Point it out!

Dropping Comments:

Click the 'Comments' tab on the right sidebar.

Select the area of the design you're addressing.

Type away! And remember: emojis, like �� and ��, elevate everything.

15.5 Using Live Review - Real-Time Genius Sharing

It's like video calling, but for your design.

Initiating a Live Review:

Go to the 'Collaborate' dropdown menu.

Select 'Start Live Review'.

Share the generated link with your mates. Let the real-time magic begin!

CHAPTER 16: MAKING IT REAL - 3D PRINTING WITH FUSION 360

16.1 Prelude: Transitioning from Digital to Physical

You've made a swanky design. Now, let's bring it into the tangible world!

16.2 Prepping Your Design for 3D Printing

Before you hit that print button:

Check Your Model's Integrity:
Go to 'Inspect' on the toolbar.
Choose 'Interference Check'. Any overlaps or gaps? Let's fix 'em!
16.3 Setting Up the Print Environment

Get your virtual workshop on point.

Enter the Print Workspace:
Head to the 'Tools' tab.
Select 'Make'. Boom! You're now in the 3D print setting. It's like stepping into a futuristic lab.
16.4 Choosing the Right Settings

Like baking, but cooler.

Selecting Print Quality:
Check the printer's settings.
Opt for high resolution for intricate designs. But hey, if you're just

prototyping, medium or low works!

16.5 Exporting to Slicer Software

Slice and dice, digitally.

Generating the STL File:
In the 'Make' workspace, click 'OK' once you're happy with the settings.
Save the STL file. Keep it somewhere safe; it's your golden ticket to 3D print town.

16.6 Tips for a Successful Print

Some golden nuggets from the pros:

Material Matters: Understand your material's properties. Flexible, durable, brittle? Choose wisely!
Optimal Orientation: The way your design sits on the printing bed matters. Think about the final product and orient for minimal supports and the best surface finish.
Patience, Young Designer: 3D printing isn't instant. It's more slow-cooking than microwave.

CHAPTER 17: THE ART OF SIMULATION - PREDICT BEFORE YOU PRODUCE

17.1 Introduction to Simulation

Before investing in materials and production, let's virtually test our design's mettle. Smart, right?

17.2 Setting Up Your Simulation Study

It's a bit like setting up dominoes, but with less risk of them all toppling over prematurely.

Choose Simulation Workspace:
Navigate to the 'Workspaces' dropdown.
Select 'Simulation'. Welcome to the command center!
17.3 Types of Simulations

There are more flavors here than at an ice-cream parlor!

Static Stress Analysis: Will your design hold up under steady, non-moving loads? Let's find out.
Modal Frequencies: Great for finding the natural vibration frequencies of your design. Perfect for musical instruments or machinery!
Thermal Analysis: Got a design that might get hot under the collar? See how it handles the heat.

17.4 Assigning Materials

Your virtual testing dummy needs the right clothes!

Accessing Material Browser:
Click on 'Manage Materials'.
Assign the right material to each part of your design. Metals? Polymers? The world's your oyster.

17.5 Applying Constraints and Loads

Tell Fusion 360 how the real world is going to treat your design.

Setting Boundaries:
In the 'Simulation' tab, find the 'Prescribed Displacements' tool. Use this to lock parts in place.
Use the 'Loads' tool to simulate forces. Gravity got you down? Apply it!

17.6 Running the Simulation

Drumroll, please...

Hit the 'Solve' button. Grab a coffee, and let Fusion 360 crunch the numbers.

17.7 Interpreting the Results

Graphs, colors, and insights, oh my!

Viewing Results:
Check out the 'Results' tab for colorful visual representations.
Focus on areas with intense colors. These might be stress points or hot spots!

CHAPTER 18: FROM DESIGN TO REALITY - A DEEP DIVE INTO CAM CAPABILITIES

18.1 What's the CAM Deal?

Imagine telling a machine how to make your design, and then it just...does it. That's CAM!

18.2 Transitioning from CAD to CAM

Just like switching from writing a novel to publishing it.

Entering the CAM Workspace:
Click on the 'Workspaces' dropdown.
Pick 'CAM'. Things might look a tad different. Don't worry, you got this!
18.3 Set Up Your Stock

Before Fusion 360 can machine anything, it needs to know what it's working with.

Define Stock Dimensions:
Choose 'Setup' from the CAM ribbon.
Under the 'Stock' tab, input the size of your material. Whether it's a block of wood or a sheet of metal, this is its time to shine!
18.4 Picking the Right Tool

It's not a one-size-fits-all deal here.

Accessing the Tool Library:
Click 'Tool Library' on the CAM ribbon.
Browse or search for the right tool for the job. Mills, drills, and lathes – oh, the choices!
18.5 Generating Toolpaths

This is where Fusion 360 plots its course!

2D vs. 3D Milling:
For flat projects, stick with 2D milling.
If your design has depth or curves, jump into 3D.
Select the tool from your library, define your paths, and hit 'OK'. Fusion 360 does the heavy lifting!
18.6 Simulation and Post Processing

Before sending your toolpaths to the machine, let's do a dry run!

Simulate Your Paths:

Click 'Simulate' on the CAM ribbon.
Watch as Fusion 360 virtually machines your design. It's like a video game, but more productive!
Post Processing:

After confirming the simulation looks good, click 'Post Process' on the CAM ribbon.
Select your machine type and save the G-code file. This is the secret language your CNC machine speaks!

CHAPTER 19:
FINISHING TOUCHES
AND FINE-TUNING

19.1 The Art of Refinement

Turning a good project into a GREAT one.

19.2 Break the Edges, Not Your Spirit

Nobody likes sharp edges. Let's smoothen them out.

Chamfers and Fillets:
Access the 'Modify' dropdown in your Design Workspace.
Choose 'Chamfer' or 'Fillet'.
Click on the edges you want to refine and adjust the values. Like giving your design a manicure!
19.3 Giving Your Design Texture

Sometimes, it's all about the feel.

Apply Textures:
Go to the 'Appearance' panel.
Browse and drag the texture you desire onto your model. Feel the groove!
19.4 Engravings to Die For

Personalize your work, because it's all about the details!

Text Engraving:
In the Sketch Workspace, select the 'Text' tool.

Write your desired text, choose a font, size it, and position it. Now, back in the CAM Workspace, set a shallow toolpath for engraving. Your design now has a signature!

19.5 Verification and Validation

Ensure your design is ready for prime time!

Interference Check:
Under the 'Inspect' dropdown, select 'Interference Check'. Choose your components and run the check. Fusion 360 will highlight any clashes. Time to troubleshoot if there are any!

19.6 Quality Over Quantity

The last step before we hit the manufacturing floor.

Tolerance Checks:
Go to the 'Inspect' dropdown.
Select 'Measure'. This allows you to check distances and ensure parts fit as intended.
Adjust your design accordingly, aiming for the Goldilocks zone: just right!

CHAPTER 20: MAKING IT MOVE - THE ANIMATION MAGIC

20.1 Introduction to Motion Studies

Making your design come alive, one frame at a time!

20.2 Creating Basic Motion Animations

Turn static into ecstatic!

Animating Components:
Access the 'Animation Workspace'.
Click 'Transform Components' and select the component to move.
Set the start and end points. Drag the playhead on the timeline to adjust the duration. Bam! Instant movie director status!
20.3 Exploded Views: It's Not as Violent as It Sounds

Breakdowns can be fun when it's about your design!

Making Exploded Views:
Still in the 'Animation Workspace', select 'Auto Explode All Components'.
Adjust distance and direction as needed. Your assembly now disassembles with flair!
20.4 Making Use of Storyboards

Your story, your rules.

Creating Storyboards:

Click the 'Storyboard' tab in the Animation Workspace.

Choose 'New Storyboard'. Think of it as creating different movie scenes!

Adjust camera views, component movements, and more to craft your story.

20.5 Rendering Your Animation

Because what's a movie without its final cut?

Getting That Perfect Render:

Click on the 'Render' tab at the bottom.

Set your desired output: Image, Turntable, or Animation.

Adjust settings like quality, background, and lighting. Then, hit 'Render'. Grab some popcorn while Fusion 360 works its magic!

20.6 Quick Tips for a Smooth Animation

Use the 'Ease In' and 'Ease Out' options for smoother component movements.

Adjust animation speed by dragging the ends of action bars on the timeline.

Use the 'Orbit' tool to change camera angles for dynamic perspectives.

CHAPTER 21: SIMULATION - BECAUSE TRIAL AND ERROR IS SO LAST CENTURY

21.1 The Why and How of Simulations

Simulations: Where your designs face the "real world" without ever leaving the screen.

21.2 Setting Up Your First Static Stress Test

You might be stressed, but make sure your design isn't!

Prepping for Static Stress:
Click on the 'Simulation Workspace'. This is your sandbox for digital reality checks.
Choose 'Static Stress' from the Study dropdown.
Select the material for your component. Fusion 360 needs to know what it's working with, after all!
21.3 Defining Constraints and Loads

Designing is no free-for-all – at least not in simulations!

Pinpointing Constraints:
Under 'Prescribed Displacements', click 'Fixed'.

Select the faces, edges, or points where your component won't move. It's like telling your design where to put its feet down!

Assigning Loads:

Click on 'Structural Loads'.

Choose the type (force, pressure, etc.) and set the magnitude. Make your design feel the weight of the (virtual) world!

21.4 Running the Simulation

Will your design stand tall or crumble? Let's find out!

Push That Button!:

Hit 'Solve'. Time for Fusion 360 to do its heavy computational lifting!

Once it's done, review the results. Color-coded visuals will show you where the maximum stress and displacement occur.

21.5 Thermal Analysis: Feeling Hot, Hot, Hot!

When things heat up, will your design keep its cool?

Setting up a Thermal Analysis:

Go back to the 'Simulation Workspace' and select 'Thermal' from the Study dropdown.

Assign materials and define heat sources. How hot can you go?

Define environmental conditions. Is your design sunbathing in the Sahara or chilling in the Arctic?

21.6 Making Sense of the Results

Deciphering the hieroglyphics of stress and strain.

Read the color gradients. Red might mean danger, while blue indicates cooler, less stressed areas.

Look at the numeric results for exact stress and displacement values. Get nerdy with those numbers!

CHAPTER 22: DYNAMIC ANALYSIS - MOVIN' & GROOVIN' IN THE DIGITAL WORLD

22.1 Introduction to Dynamic Analysis

Like a dance floor for your designs, let's see how they move and shake when the rhythm gets going.

22.2 Setting Up a Modal Frequency Study

Your design's got vibes, let's tune into its frequency.

Entering the Modal Realm:
Navigate to 'Simulation Workspace'.
Opt for 'Modal Frequency' from the Study dropdown.
Assign the materials for each part. Fusion's gotta know what tunes we're jamming to!
22.3 Defining Boundary Conditions

Give your design some boundaries (not the emotional kind, don't worry).

Setting the Stage:
Under 'Boundary Conditions', click 'Pin'.
Highlight the areas of your design that need to stay put. You're the puppet master here!
22.4 Assigning Dynamic Loads

Time to shake things up a bit! ��

Creating Motion:
Click 'Dynamic Loads'.
Pick the type of motion (oscillating, random, etc.) and its magnitude. Turn up the volume on that bass!
22.5 Running the Modal Analysis

Does your design dance like Jagger or is it more of a wallflower?

Let's Boogie:
Hit 'Solve'. Fusion's gonna play DJ now!
Review your results. The graphical patterns show the frequencies and modes of vibration. Bet you didn't think you'd be a dance judge today!
22.6 Interpreting Vibrational Modes

Breaking down the boogie.

Each mode represents a unique dance move or vibration of your design.
Color representations help identify areas with maximum motion.
If it's red and rocking, you've got a headbanger!

CHAPTER 23: ADVANCED RENDERING - MAKE YOUR DESIGNS POP, LOCK, AND DROP!

23.1 Unleashing the Power of the Appearance Toolbox

First, you've got to dress to impress.

Picking Out the Threads:
Go to the 'Render Workspace'.
Use 'Appearance' on the toolbar. Fusion's wardrobe is vast!
Browse materials, colors, and textures. Sequins or satin, what's your design's style?
23.2 The Art of Lighting

Like any good photoshoot, lighting is key.

Spotlight on Your Design:
Head to 'Scene Settings'. It's like setting the stage for a Broadway show!
Adjust 'Brightness' and 'Contrast'. You're the director now.
Play with different light sources. Sun, lamps, ambient light - make sure your design's good side is showing!
23.3 Perspective & Camera Angles

Getting all Spielberg on your projects!

Directing the Shot:
Zoom, pan, and orbit. Move around like you're floating in space!
Set 'Depth of Field'. Blur out the haters and focus on what's important!
23.4 Decals - Tattooing Your Design

Give your design some personality!

Tat It Up:
Click 'Decals' in the Appearance tab.
Upload your image or choose from Fusion's gallery.
Adjust size and position. Whether it's a tiny heart or a fierce dragon, make it count!
23.5 Rendering that Masterpiece

Aaaaand action!

Roll the Cameras:
Go to 'In-Canvas Render'. Let's get cinematic!
Choose the quality and duration. Like picking film for an old-school camera.
Click 'Start'. Time for Fusion to work its Hollywood magic!

CHAPTER 24: ANIMATIONS - BRINGING YOUR DESIGN TO LIFE

24.1 The Basics of Fusion 360 Animation

Animation isn't just for cartoons! Here's how to make your design do a little dance.

Starting Simple:
Open the 'Animation Workspace'. It's where the magic happens!
Select 'Storyboard'. Think of it as your movie timeline.
Drag parts in the canvas to create movement. Watch them slide and glide!
24.2 Adjusting Animation Time

Remember, timing is everything!

Time's a-Ticking:
On your storyboard, adjust the 'Time Slider'.
Extend or reduce the duration as needed. Every second counts!
Play it back. Smooth as butter or needs a tweak?
24.3 Capturing Your Design's Best Angles

Because your creation deserves its best shot.

Camera, Action!:
Right-click on the timeline. Select 'New Camera View'.

Set your design's pose. Vogue! Strike that pose!

Preview with 'Play'. How's that for a view?

24.4 Animating Components

A little movement never hurt anyone!

Move It, Groove It:

Select a component. Any part you want to boogie.

Click 'Animate'. Let the dance begin!

Adjust paths and directions. Make it twirl, jump, or shimmy!

24.5 Adding Realistic Transitions

And now, for the finishing touches.

Smoothing Things Out:

Go to 'Transitions' in the toolbar.

Select 'Ease In' or 'Ease Out'. It's like adding flair to your dance moves!

Adjust the curve for perfect flow. Smooth operator!

CHAPTER 25: SIMULATION – TESTING YOUR DESIGN'S METTLE

25.1 Why Simulate? An Overview

Here's why you should put your designs through the wringer.

The Why and the Wise:
Predict product performance. Because nobody likes bad surprises!
Improve product longevity. Go the distance!
Save resources and time. Less trial, less error!

25.2 Setting Up Your First Simulation

Your design's first rite of passage. Let's dive in!

Getting the Ball Rolling:
Switch to the 'Simulation Workspace'. The stage is set!
Choose a study type. Static stress? Thermal? The world's your oyster!
Assign materials to your components. Steel? Rubber? Choose your warrior!

25.3 Boundary Conditions and Loads

This is where you set the ground rules. No cheating!

Marking the Boundaries:
Click on 'Boundary Conditions' in the toolbar.

THE ULTIMATE GUIDE TO FUSION 360: 2024 EDITION

Fix or pin parts of your design. No moving out of turn!
Apply loads. Push it, pull it, twist it. Challenge accepted!
25.4 Running the Simulation

Now, watch your design sweat it out!

Crunch Those Numbers:
Click on 'Solve' in the toolbar. Go, Fusion 360, go!
Choose local or cloud solve. Sky's the limit, literally!
Monitor the progress. Grab some popcorn!
25.5 Interpreting Results

Reading between the lines (and colors).

Decoding the Magic:
Check out the color-coded results. Red-hot or cool blue?
Zoom in on problem areas. Oops, see a crack?
Tweak your design based on insights. Iterate, iterate, iterate!

CHAPTER 26: RENDERING – BRINGING YOUR DESIGN TO LIFE

26.1 The Whys and Hows of Rendering

Why settle for flat when you can have fab?

Rendering Realness:
Gives a real-world look to your designs.
Helps in marketing and presentations. Because first impressions count!
Facilitates design communication. Let the visuals do the talking!
26.2 Setting the Stage: The Rendering Workspace

Before you paint, set up the canvas!

Switch It Up:
Move to the 'Render Workspace'. It's showtime!
Familiarize yourself with the toolbar. Tools are your paintbrushes here!
26.3 Lighting and Scenes

Good lighting can be the difference between meh and WOW!

Bright Ideas:
Navigate to the 'Scene Settings'. Lighting, camera, action!
Choose a lighting scheme. Sunrise, studio, neon... mood matters!

Select your background. Beach, workshop, outer space? Sky's the limit!

26.4 Materials and Textures

That touch-me feel? It starts here.

Getting the Feel Right:
Click on 'Appearance' in the toolbar. Feel the vibe!
Drag and drop materials onto your design. Glossy, matte, metallic, oh my!
Adjust textures for added depth. Give it that grain, gloss, or grunge!

26.5 Capturing the Moment: The Final Render

The grand reveal!

Snapshot Sensation:
Adjust camera angles. Find your design's best side (hint: all of them!).
Set the quality and resolution. Go HD or go home!
Click 'Render'. Sit back and watch the magic unfold!

CHAPTER 27: COLLABORATION – TEAMWORK IN FUSION 360

27.1 The Power of Teamwork

They say "two heads are better than one", and Fusion 360's collaboration features are all about that!

Benefits of Collaborative Design:
Faster problem-solving – more brains, more ideas!
Enhanced creativity – diverse minds bring diverse designs!
Streamlined communication – no more "lost in translation" moments.

27.2 Setting Up Your Fusion 360 Team

It's like forming your own Avengers squad, but for design!

Forming the Squad:
Head to 'Team Hub'. Time to gather the heroes!
Invite members using their emails. Every Iron Man needs a Captain America!
Set roles and permissions. Remember, with great power comes great responsibility!

27.3 Sharing and Commenting

The Fusion 360 chatroom!

Speak Your Design Mind:
Open your design and click 'Share'. Spread the design love!
Use the 'Comment' tool. It's like texting, but for design geeks!
Tag team members. Hey @TonyStark, check out this arc reactor design!

27.4 Version Control and History

Mistakes happen. That's why we have the time stone...err, version control!

The Time Machine:
Access the 'History' tab. It's like a time-travel diary for your design!
Create and name versions. V1, V2, V-OMG-THIS-IS-AWESOME!
Revert to previous versions if needed. It's like CTRL+Z for life!

27.5 Live Review Sessions

It's brainstorming time, but make it virtual!

Brainwaves in Sync:
Click on 'Live Review'. The design conference room, but comfier!
Invite team members. No need for suits, PJs will do!
Discuss, draw, and design in real-time. The magic of technology!

CHAPTER 28: SIMULATION – REALITY TESTING IN FUSION 360

28.1 Why Simulate?

Before deploying Iron Man's suit, Tony Stark made sure it won't buckle under pressure, right? That's why we simulate!

The Importance of Simulation:
Save money: Test virtually, not physically.
Boost safety: Predict and solve potential risks.
Enhance design: Make informed improvements.
28.2 Preparing Your Model for Simulation

You wouldn't go to a battle without armor. Similarly, prep your model first!

Model Ready-Up:
Start with a clean design. A clutter-free workspace is a mind at peace.
Simplify the geometry. Keep what's essential.
Patch all open faces. Seal the deal!
28.3 Types of Simulations

Different strokes for different folks!

Choosing the Right One:

Static Stress: Checks if your design can handle the load without moving. Great for stationary objects.
Modal Frequencies: For all things that vibrate. Tuning forks, anyone?
Thermal Analysis: If it's going to get hot, this one's for you!
28.4 Running the Simulation

Ready. Set. Simulate!

Execute the Plan:
Head over to the 'Simulation' workspace. Your virtual testing ground!
Apply materials to your model. Is it steel? Rubber? Vibranium?!
Assign constraints and loads. Tell Fusion how and where to push and pull.
Hit 'Solve'. Fusion does the heavy lifting while you grab a coffee!
28.5 Interpreting the Results

Those pretty colors have meaning!

Reading the Rainbow:
Understand the color scale. From cool blue (all good) to fiery red (uh-oh).
Examine displacement plots. How much did it move?
Check the safety factor. Always aim for safety!

CHAPTER 29: CAM (COMPUTER-AIDED MANUFACTURING) - TURNING DESIGNS INTO REALITY

29.1 What's CAM and Why Care?

A sculptor has a chisel. You, dear Fusion artist, have CAM!

CAM Decoded:
A bridge from design to physical product.
Use your 3D model to guide machine tools.
Produce components with laser-sharp precision.
29.2 Setting up your Workspace

Just like a chef's mise en place, set your digital workshop!

Getting Things Ready:
Navigate to the 'CAM' workspace.
Ensure your design is finalized. Once CAM starts, no going back!
Define your machine. Tell Fusion which machine you'll be using.
29.3 Toolpaths - Your Roadmap to Success

Every masterpiece needs a plan.

Defining Your Path:

2D Milling: Best for flat components.
3D Milling: For those intricate 3D parts.
Turning: Lathes love this! Great for cylindrical parts.
Adjust cutting parameters: Depth, speed, and step-over. Make sure to avoid tool collisions!
29.4 Post Processing - Speak Your Machine's Language

Every machine has its own dialect.

Make Fusion and Your Machine Talk:
Click on 'Post Process' in the CAM workspace.
Choose your machine's post-processor from Fusion's vast library.
Set your configurations: Which coordinate system? Any specific codes?
Save and export your G-code. That's your machine's playbook!
29.5 Safety First!

You're a creator, not a destroyer. Safety is key.

Smart Practices:
Always run a simulation before actual milling.
Wear safety gear. Goggles, gloves, and ear protection.
Keep your workspace clean. A tidy space = fewer accidents.

CHAPTER 30: COLLABORATIVE DESIGN IN FUSION 360 - TEAMWORK MAKES THE DREAM WORK

30.1 Introduction to Collaboration

When multiple minds combine, the design sky is the limit.

Why Collaborate?
Share ideas and get instant feedback.
Tackle complex projects with a team.
Real-time collaboration means no more back-and-forth emails.
30.2 Setting up Your Team

Before the design collaboration begins, let's bring everyone on board.

Getting Started:
Head to the 'Team Hub' on the Fusion 360 dashboard.
Click 'Invite Members' and enter their email addresses.
Assign roles: Can they edit, view, or comment?
30.3 Live Collaboration - Designing Together, From Anywhere

No need to be in the same room to bring an idea to life.

Making It Happen:
Open your design in Fusion 360.
Click on 'Share Link' in the top-right corner.
Choose whether collaborators can only view or edit.
Watch in real-time as your team collaborates. See who's doing what, thanks to colored cursors.

30.4 Using Comments and Feedback

Because constructive feedback can turn a good design into a great one.

Effective Communication:
Click on the 'Comment' tab in the right panel.
Highlight the design area you're referring to and type your feedback.
Use '@' to mention team members and get their attention.
Resolve comments once they've been addressed to keep things organized.

30.5 Version Control - The Magic of Mistake Proofing

It's okay to mess up; Fusion has got your back!

Keeping Track:
Fusion automatically saves versions as you work.
To view or revert to a previous version, head to the 'Data Panel', find your project, and click on the clock icon.
Choose the version you want to revisit and marvel at the power of tech!

CHAPTER 31: RENDERING IN FUSION 360 – MAKING YOUR DESIGN SHINE

31.1 The Power of Rendering

Rendering can transform a simple 3D model into a lifelike representation, making it easier for stakeholders to visualize the final product.

Why Render?
Visualize the final product.
Create marketing material and presentations.
Validate design aesthetics before manufacturing.
31.2 Setting Up for Rendering

Preparation is key.

Choosing the Right Workspace:
From the Fusion 360 workspace dropdown, select 'Render'.
This switches your design tools to rendering tools, optimizing the environment for visual magic.
31.3 Applying Materials

The right texture can make a world of difference.

Steps to Apply Materials:
In the Render workspace, click on the 'Appearance' icon.

Browse the library to find the desired material.

Drag and drop the material onto your model's part or surface.

31.4 Setting the Scene with Lighting

Good lighting is the difference between an average and a stunning render.

Adjusting the Lighting:

In the 'Scene Settings' panel, adjust the brightness and contrast to set the mood.

Choose the type of environment: studio, outdoor, indoor, etc. Each provides a unique lighting setup.

Use HDR environments for realistic reflections and ambiance.

31.5 Camera Angles and Perspectives

Because showcasing your design from its best angle matters.

Setting the Perfect Angle:

Use the 'Orbit', 'Pan', and 'Zoom' tools to find the best perspective.

Save specific camera views for easy access using the 'Named Views' option.

31.6 The Rendering Process

Time to bring it all to life.

Starting Your Render:

Click on 'In-Canvas Render' for a quick preview directly in Fusion 360.

For higher quality, select 'Render' from the toolbar and choose either 'Cloud Render' or 'Local Render'.

Adjust quality settings: The higher the quality, the longer the render, but the results are worth the wait!

CHAPTER 32: SIMULATION IN FUSION 360 – TESTING YOUR DESIGNS VIRTUALLY

32.1 Understanding the Importance of Simulation

Simulations allow designers to virtually test their models, ensuring they're both functional and safe.

Why Use Simulation?
Predict performance and behavior of designs.
Identify potential issues early, saving time and money.
Optimize designs for real-world conditions.
32.2 Setting Up Your Simulation

Let's prepare your design for a simulation run.

Entering the Simulation Workspace:
From the main dropdown menu in Fusion 360, select 'Simulation'.
Your tools are now specifically tailored to conduct simulations.
32.3 Types of Simulations

Fusion 360 offers a plethora of simulation types.

Common Types and Their Uses:

Static Stress: Analyzes force distributions and displacements in stationary objects.

Thermal Stress: Studies the effects of temperature variations.

Modal Frequencies: Explores an object's natural vibration frequencies.

Event Simulation: Evaluates the impacts of sudden or periodic events on a design.

32.4 Applying Constraints and Loads

For a successful simulation, setting realistic constraints and loads is paramount.

Applying Constraints:

Under the 'Setup' panel, click on 'Fixed' to select the portions of the design to remain stationary.

'Pinned' and 'Slider' are other constraint options for specific movement limitations.

Setting Loads:

Click on the 'Force' or 'Pressure' option, depending on the design's interaction with its environment.

Input values for magnitude and direction.

32.5 Running the Simulation

Once everything is set, you're ready to simulate!

Starting Your Simulation:

Click on the 'Solve' option in the toolbar.

Select the desired type of study, like 'Static Stress' or 'Thermal Analysis'.

Choose either 'Cloud Solve' for faster results or 'Local Solve' to run the simulation on your machine.

32.6 Analyzing Results

Understanding the results is crucial for refining your design.

Interpreting the Data:

Once the simulation is complete, Fusion 360 will display color-coded visual results.

Study the 'Displacement', 'Stress', and 'Safety Factor' plots to gauge performance.

Adjust and re-run simulations as necessary to achieve optimal outcomes.

CHAPTER 33: COLLABORATIVE FEATURES IN FUSION 360 – WORKING TOGETHER SEAMLESSLY

33.1 The Power of Collaboration

The ability to work together in real-time, even from disparate geographical locations, is one of Fusion 360's distinguishing characteristics.

Why Collaboration is Essential:
Speed up design iterations and approval processes.
Foster team synergy and unity.
Access multiple viewpoints to refine and perfect designs.

33.2 Setting Up Your Fusion Team

Before diving into collaboration, it's essential to set up your Fusion team.

Creating a Fusion Team:
Navigate to the Fusion 360 Data Panel.
Click on 'New Team' and input your desired team name.

Invite members by entering their email addresses. They will receive an invitation link.

33.3 Real-Time Design Collaboration

Gone are the days of emailing CAD files back and forth!

Starting a Collaborative Session:

Open the desired design in Fusion 360.
Click on the 'Collaborate' icon on the top right (it looks like two avatars).
Invite team members to join the session by entering their usernames or email addresses.
Collaborative Tools at Your Fingertips:

Shared Cursor: See where team members are pointing or making changes in real-time.
Live Chat: Communicate directly within Fusion 360 without needing external apps.
Annotations: Leave notes or mark areas directly on the design for team members to review.
33.4 Version Control and History

Keeping track of changes and revisions is a breeze with Fusion's built-in tools.

Accessing Version History:

In the Data Panel, locate the design you're interested in.
Click on the 'Version' number, which will show a dropdown of all saved versions.
Each version displays the author, date, and any accompanying notes.
Creating a Version Milestone:

Click on the 'Save' icon.
A window will pop up prompting you for notes about the changes you made.
Mark important versions as milestones to highlight their

significance in the project's evolution.

33.5 Sharing & Exporting Collaborative Projects

For stakeholders outside your team or for presentations, Fusion 360 allows secure sharing and exporting options.

Sharing Your Design:

Right-click on your design in the Data Panel.
Select 'Share Public Link.' This link can be viewed by anyone, even without a Fusion 360 account.
Adjust link settings as desired, such as making the link view-only or allowing downloads.
Exporting Your Collaborative Work:

Right-click on your project.
Select 'Export.' Fusion 360 supports various formats, such as .F3D, .IGES, .STL, and more.

CHAPTER 34:
BRINGING YOUR
DESIGNS TO LIFE
WITH 3D PRINTING

34.1 Introduction to 3D Printing with Fusion 360

3D printing is a revolutionary method that turns digital 3D models into tangible objects. With Fusion 360, you're not just limited to creating and simulating designs; you can prepare them for 3D printing directly from the platform!

34.2 Preparing Your Model for 3D Printing

Before sending your design to a 3D printer, it's crucial to ensure it's optimized.

Inspecting Your Design:

Rotate and pan around your design to visually inspect for any inconsistencies.
Use the "Inspect" tool to measure dimensions and ensure they match your desired specs.
Use the "Analysis" tool to detect and highlight any potential problematic areas.
Hollowing Your Model:

To save material, you might want to print a hollow version of your model.

Select "Modify" > "Shell".
Click on the face you want to open and set your desired wall thickness.

34.3 Slicing in Fusion 360

While Fusion 360 doesn't directly slice models, it prepares them to be easily managed by slicing software.

Exporting for Slicing:
Click on "File" > "3D Print".
Ensure the "Preview Mesh" option is selected.
Adjust the refinement settings based on your printer's capabilities.
Click "OK" and save the .STL file.

34.4 Choosing the Right Material and Printer

Different projects require different materials, from PLA and ABS to specialized filaments.

Material Considerations:
PLA: Biodegradable and easy to use. Ideal for prototypes and non-functional parts.
ABS: Durable and temperature-resistant. Suited for functional parts.
TPU: Flexible and resilient. Great for parts requiring elasticity.
Printer Selection:
While Fusion 360 is agnostic to printer brands, ensure your printer is compatible with the exported .STL files and can handle your chosen material.

34.5 Post-Processing Your Print

After your design has been printed, some post-processing steps can enhance its appearance and functionality.

Sanding:

Begin with coarse sandpaper (around 200-grit) for initial smoothing.
Progressively use finer grits (up to 1000 or higher) for a polished

finish.

Painting and Sealing:

Apply a primer suitable for your material.
Use acrylic or spray paint for coloring.
Seal with a clear coat for added protection and sheen.

CHAPTER 35: INTEGRATING ELECTRONICS WITH FUSION 360

35.1 Introduction to Electronics in Fusion 360

Fusion 360 isn't just a powerhouse for mechanical design; it also boasts integrated electronics design capabilities. This allows engineers and designers to bring together mechanical designs and electronic layouts within a unified environment.

35.2 Setting Up Your Electronics Workspace

To access the electronics workspace:

Click on the workspace dropdown in the top-left corner.
Choose "Electronics."
The interface shifts to display tools and panels relevant to electronics design, including schematics and PCB layouts.

35.3 Designing Your First Schematic

Starting a New Schematic:

Click on "File" > "New Schematic."
Familiarize yourself with the schematic editor, noting tools like "Add Component" and "Wire."
Adding Components:

Click on "Add Component."

Navigate the extensive library to find desired components. You can search by component name or number.

Click to place each component on the schematic grid.

Connecting Components:

Select the "Wire" tool.

Click on the pin of one component and drag to another component's pin to establish a connection.

35.4 Transitioning from Schematic to PCB Layout

Once your schematic is complete, it's time to transition to the PCB layout:

Click "Design" > "Create PCB."

Fusion 360 will attempt to auto-arrange components, but manual adjustments might be necessary.

Use the "Route" tool to draw connections between components based on the schematic.

35.5 Finalizing and Exporting for Manufacturing

With the PCB layout complete, you're ready to prepare for manufacturing:

Checking the Design:

Click "Design" > "Design Rule Check." Address any issues or conflicts Fusion 360 identifies.

Generating Gerber Files:

Click "File" > "Export" > "Gerber."

Configure the settings as needed and ensure all layers you wish to include are selected.

Click "OK" to generate the files, which can be sent to a PCB manufacturer.

CHAPTER 36: COLLABORATIVE DESIGNING IN FUSION 360

36.1 The Power of Collaboration in Fusion 360

In the modern design world, collaboration is more crucial than ever. Whether you're working with team members in the same office or from different parts of the globe, Fusion 360's collaborative tools ensure seamless integration and efficient teamwork.

36.2 Setting Up Your Fusion Team Hub

Accessing the Fusion Team Hub: From the Fusion 360 dashboard, click on the "Collaborate" tab.
Creating a New Project: Click "New Project" and provide a name and description. This will be your central hub for shared files, version history, and collaborative discussions.
36.3 Inviting Team Members

Navigate to your project in Fusion Team Hub.
Click on the "Members" tab.
Click "Invite" and enter the email addresses of your teammates.
Set their access levels: Viewer, Editor, or Admin.
Click "Send Invitation." Your teammates will receive an email prompting them to join the project.

36.4 Collaborative Designing in Real-Time

Opening a Shared Document: From the project dashboard, select a document to open.

Real-Time Editing: Multiple users can work on the same design simultaneously. Edits made by one user will be instantly visible to others. User icons indicate who is currently working on the design.

Commenting: Use the "Comment" tool to leave feedback or ask questions directly on the design. Mention team members using "@" followed by their username to notify them.

36.5 Version and Revision Control

Saving and Versioning: Each time you save your design, Fusion 360 creates a new version. This allows you to track changes and revert to previous versions if needed.

Accessing Version History: Click on the version number at the top of the screen. This displays a list of all saved versions. You can preview, promote, or open any version.

Promoting a Version: If you wish to revert to a previous version, simply click "Promote" next to the desired version. This will set it as the current version, but no data from newer versions will be lost.

36.6 Final Tips for Collaborative Success

Regularly Sync: Make sure you're working on the latest version of a design. Before starting, sync your data.

Clear Communication: Use the commenting system efficiently. Clear, concise feedback ensures everyone stays on the same page.

Set Boundaries: While collaboration is vital, too many edits can be chaotic. Establish clear roles for each team member to ensure a smooth workflow.

CHAPTER 37: ADVANCED SIMULATION AND ANALYSIS IN FUSION 360

37.1 Understanding the Need for Simulation

Simulation is an integral part of the design process. It allows you to anticipate and rectify potential failures, stresses, and inefficiencies in your design without having to create physical prototypes. With Fusion 360's advanced simulation tools, you can ensure that your designs not only look good but also perform optimally in real-world conditions.

37.2 Setting Up for Simulation

Select the Workspace: From the Fusion 360 workspace dropdown, select "Simulation."
Choose the Study Type: Fusion 360 offers various study types like static stress, modal frequencies, thermal stresses, and more. Select the one that best suits your needs.
Assign Material: Ensure that your design parts have materials assigned to them. Fusion 360's material library provides properties needed for accurate simulations.
37.3 Running a Static Stress Analysis

Fixing Your Model: Use the "Fixed" constraint to specify which parts of your model are stationary.

Load Application: Use the "Structural Load" tool to apply forces to your design.

Meshing: Click on the "Generate Mesh" option. This divides your design into smaller elements, preparing it for simulation.

Run Simulation: Click on "Solve" to begin the static stress analysis.

37.4 Interpreting Results

Accessing Result Overview: Once the simulation is complete, Fusion 360 will display a summary of the results.

Stress Analysis: Look for areas in your design that exceed the material's yield strength. These are potential failure points.

Displacement Analysis: This shows how much each part of your design will move under the applied loads.

Safety Factor: A critical metric indicating if your design meets the required safety benchmarks. A value below 1 indicates potential failure.

37.5 Making Design Modifications

Based on the simulation results:

Reinforcing Stress Points: If certain areas show excessive stress, consider adding more material or changing the geometry to distribute the stress more evenly.

Reducing Material: If the safety factor is much higher than needed, you might be able to reduce material in some areas, making your design more cost-effective.

Rerun Simulations: After making modifications, run the simulation again to validate the changes.

37.6 Final Thoughts on Simulation

Fusion 360's simulation capabilities provide designers with a powerful tool to optimize their designs. By regularly incorporating simulation into your design workflow, you can create more durable, efficient, and cost-effective products.

CHAPTER 38: INTEGRATING 3D PRINTING WITH FUSION 360

38.1 The Revolution of 3D Printing

In recent years, 3D printing, also known as additive manufacturing, has changed the landscape of design and manufacturing. Fusion 360 seamlessly integrates with this technology, allowing designers to take their creations from the screen to reality with ease.

38.2 Preparing Your Model for 3D Printing

Before exporting your design for 3D printing:

Check Model Integrity: Ensure that your design is watertight with no holes or gaps. Fusion 360's "Inspect" tool can help identify and fix any discrepancies.
Simplify Your Model: To avoid printing errors and to save time and material, try to minimize overly complex geometries and thin walls.
38.3 Setting Up the Print Utility

Select the 3D Print Tool: Click on the "Make" icon in Fusion 360's toolbar and choose "3D Print."
Choose the Object: Select the object you wish to print.

Refinement Options: You can choose to send the design as is or send it to a print utility or slicing software for further refinement.

38.4 Exporting for a 3D Printer

File Format: Most 3D printers use the STL file format. Ensure that this option is selected in the "Output" dropdown.

Refinement in Slicing Software: After exporting the design as an STL file, import it into your slicing software (like Cura or PrusaSlicer). This software will allow you to choose print settings, generate supports, and more.

Exporting G-Code: The slicing software will generate a G-Code file that can be loaded into the 3D printer. This file contains all the instructions needed to print the model.

38.5 Optimizing Print Settings

Layer Height: Smaller layer heights (e.g., 0.1mm) provide more detail but take longer to print. Larger heights (e.g., 0.3mm) are quicker but less detailed.

Infill: Choose a percentage of infill to balance between strength and material usage.

Supports: For overhanging parts of your design, enable supports to prevent sagging during printing.

Printing Speed: Faster speeds can reduce print time but may affect print quality.

38.6 Post-Processing Your 3D Prints

Once your design is printed:

Remove Supports: Carefully break away or cut any supports using pliers or a craft knife.

Sanding: Use sandpaper to smooth out any rough edges or visible layer lines.

Painting and Finishing: Enhance the appearance of your model with paints, sealants, or other finishes to give it a professional touch.

38.7 Conclusion

Fusion 360 and 3D printing are a match made in design heaven.

The ability to quickly prototype, iterate, and finalize designs has never been more accessible. As 3D printing technology continues to advance, the integration with Fusion 360 ensures that designers are always at the forefront of innovation.

CHAPTER 39:
COLLABORATION
AND SHARING IN
FUSION 360

39.1 The Need for Collaboration in Modern Design

In the contemporary design ecosystem, collaboration is more than a luxury – it's a necessity. Distributed teams, client feedback, and rapid iterations make tools that support collaboration vital.

39.2 Setting Up Fusion Team

Fusion Team enhances collaborative efforts by allowing multiple users to access and co-edit projects.

Creating a New Team: Navigate to the Fusion 360 Data Panel and click on the "Fusion Team" dropdown. Select "New Team" and provide a suitable name.
Inviting Members: Once your team is established, invite members by their email addresses. Assign roles (Admin, Editor, Viewer) based on their responsibilities.
39.3 Sharing Designs with External Stakeholders

Not everyone in your project might have Fusion 360. Here's how to share with them:

Public Link: Right-click on the design file and select "Share Public Link." This creates a view-only link accessible by anyone.

Exporting Files: Fusion 360 supports various formats, including .STL, .OBJ, .DWG, and more. You can export and share these as needed.

39.4 Real-Time Design Reviews with Fusion Team

Starting a Live Review: Select the design, click on the "Share" icon, and choose "Live Review."

Navigational Tools: Use the provided tools to pan, zoom, and rotate during the review.

Annotations: Participants can drop comments and feedback directly on the design.

39.5 Version Control: Keeping Track of Iterations

One of Fusion 360's strengths is its built-in version control:

Accessing Version History: Right-click on a design and choose "Version History." This will show all saved iterations of the design.

Promoting a Version: If you wish to revert to an older design, you can promote that version to be the latest.

39.6 Conclusion

Collaboration tools in Fusion 360 ensure that distance and varied software proficiency aren't barriers in today's interconnected world. Sharing, reviewing, and iterating become streamlined, ensuring a smoother design experience.

CHAPTER 40: CUSTOMIZING FUSION 360 FOR YOUR WORKFLOW

40.1 Why Customization Matters

Fusion 360 is robust out of the box, but the beauty lies in tailoring it to fit your unique needs.

40.2 Setting Up Your Workspace

Changing UI Color: Navigate to your profile, choose preferences, and under "General," you'll find the "UI Theme" option. Choose between light and dark themes.
Customizing the Toolbar: Drag and drop your most-used tools to the toolbar for quick access.
40.3 Keyboard Shortcuts

Default Shortcuts: Fusion 360 has pre-defined keyboard shortcuts like "S" for sketch or "D" for dimension.
Creating Custom Shortcuts: Navigate to Preferences → Customizations → Keyboard Shortcuts. Assign your desired key combinations.
40.4 Scripting and Add-ons

Accessing the Add-on Store: Via the "Tools" menu, select "Add-ons" to browse available scripts and extensions.

Writing Your Own Script: If you're adept at Python or JavaScript, you can create custom scripts. Use Fusion 360's API documentation as a reference.

40.5 Conclusion

Tailoring Fusion 360 ensures it works for you, not the other way around. From UI tweaks to powerful scripts, customization makes Fusion 360 truly your own.

CHAPTER 41: THE FUTURE OF FUSION 360 AND CONCLUSION

41.1 Staying Updated

Autodesk frequently updates Fusion 360, introducing new features and enhancements. Always ensure you're running the latest version.

41.2 Engaging with the Fusion 360 Community

Forums and Tutorials: Autodesk has an active community. Engage in forums, watch tutorials, and even attend webinars.
Feedback and Suggestions: Autodesk values user feedback. If you encounter issues or have ideas for improvement, report them.

41.3 Final Thoughts

Fusion 360 is more than just a CAD/CAM tool; it's a comprehensive design ecosystem. Its capabilities, combined with a dedication to learning and adapting, promise a future of limitless design possibilities. Whether you're a hobbyist or a professional, the journey with Fusion 360 is ever-evolving, ensuring you're always at the forefront of design innovation.

End of "The Ultimate Guide to Fusion 360: 2024 Edition." We hope this guide serves as a valuable resource in your Fusion 360 journey. Always keep exploring, learning, and innovating.